IT'S COOL TO LEARN ABOUT COUNTRIES

Social Studies Explorer

BRAZIL

◆ by Vicky Franchino

CHERRY LAKE PUBLISHING • ANN ARBOR, MICHIGAN

CHERRY LAKE
Publishing

Published in the United States of America
by Cherry Lake Publishing
Ann Arbor, Michigan
www.cherrylakepublishing.com

Content Adviser: Luciano Tosta, PhD, Assistant Professor of Brazilian Literature and Culture,
University of Illinois at Urbana-Champaign

Book design: The Design Lab

Photo credits: Cover and page 1, ©Giancarlo Liguori/Shutterstock, Inc.; Brazil stamp,
©iStockphoto.com/karma_pema; page 4, ©Celso Diniz/Shutterstock, Inc.; page 6, ©iStockphoto.
com/AM29; page 7, ©iStockphoto.com/milehightraveler; page 8, ©Frontpage/Shutterstock,
Inc.; page 10, ©jbor/Shutterstock, Inc.; page 11, ©iStockphoto.com/naphtalina; page 13,
©iStockphoto.com/wsfurlan; page 14, ©Marcelo Rudini/Alamy; page 15, ©David R. Frazier
Photolibrary, Inc./Alamy; page 17, ©iStockphoto.com/lucato; page 18, ©Picture Contact/
Alamy; page 19, ©Dave Sherman/Alamy; page 21, ©Balthasar Thomass/Alamy; page 23,
©Eye Ubiquitous/Alamy; page 24, ©iStockphoto.com/LuBueno; page 25, ©Steven Wright/
Shutterstock, Inc.; page 26, ©ostill/Shutterstock, Inc.; page 29, ©Jon Arnold Images Ltd/Alamy;
page 30, ©istockphoto.com/Brasil2; page 33, ©BrazilPhotos.com/Alamy; page 34, ©Edward
Parker/Alamy; page 35, ©Neil Tingle/Alamy; pages 38 and 40, ©Vinicius Tupinamba/
Shutterstock, Inc.; page 39, ©Jakub Pavlinec/Shutterstock, Inc.; page 41, ©Andre Seale/Alamy;
page 42, ©iStockphoto.com/LiciaR; page 45, ©mangostock/Shutterstock, Inc.

Library of Congress Cataloging-in-Publication Data
Franchino, Vicky.
    It's cool to learn about countries—Brazil/by Vicky Franchino.
        p. cm.—(Social studies explorer)
    Includes bibliographical references and index.
    ISBN-13: 978-1-60279-827-4 (lib. bdg.)
    ISBN-10: 1-60279-827-3 (lib. bdg.)
1. Brazil—Juvenile literature.
I. Title. II. Title: Brazil. III. Series.
    F2508.5.F69 2011
    981—dc22   2009048069

Cherry Lake Publishing would like to acknowledge the work of The Partnership for 21st
Century Skills. Please visit www.21stcenturyskills.org for more information.

Printed in the United States of America
Corporate Graphics Inc.
July 2010
CLFA07

TABLE OF CONTENTS

CHAPTER ONE
Welcome to Brazil! 4

CHAPTER TWO
Business and Government in Brazil 13

CHAPTER THREE
Meet the People 21

CHAPTER FOUR
Let's Celebrate! 29

CHAPTER FIVE
Time to Eat! 38

Glossary 46
For More Information......47
Index 48
About the Author 48

WELCOME TO BRAZIL!

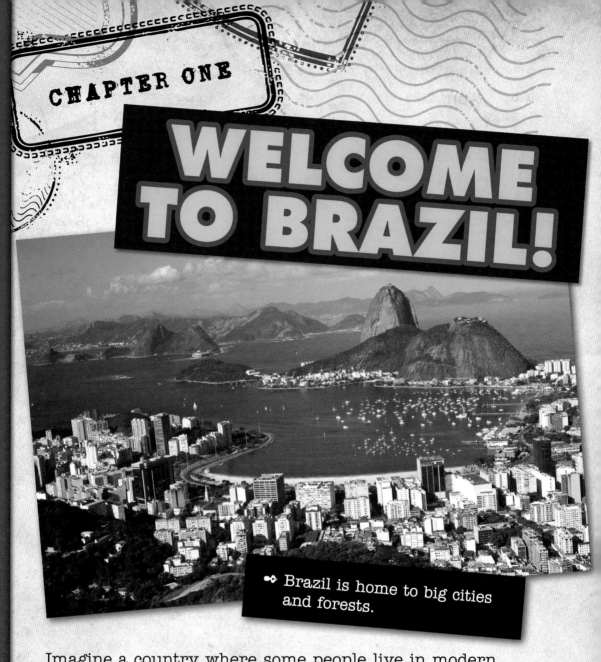

✦ Brazil is home to big cities and forests.

Imagine a country where some people live in modern skyscrapers and others live in small villages or rainforest huts. A country where Christmas comes in the summer. A country where there are more kinds of plants and animals than you can find anywhere else on Earth. That country is Brazil!

Brazil is the fifth largest country in the world. Only Russia, Canada, the United States, and China are bigger. It spans 3,287,612.4 square miles (8,514,877 square kilometers). That is a bit smaller than the United States. Brazil is located in South America. It's the biggest country on that continent. It is so large that it touches every country in South America except for Chile and Ecuador. Brazil has five different regions: the north, the central west, the northeast, the south, and the southeast.

➥ Brazil is the largest country in South America..

➥ The Amazon River twists and turns through Brazil's rainforest.

In the northern part of Brazil you'll find the highest point in the country, Pico da Neblina. It is 9,888 feet (3,014 meters) high. You'll also find the Amazon River in northern Brazil. The Amazon is the second longest river in the world. It is more than 4,000 miles (6,437 kilometers) long. Approximately half of it flows through Brazil.

Amazonia, the world's largest rainforest, is here, too. This rainforest is an exciting place to visit. It's filled with unusual birds, animals, insects, and plants.

piranha

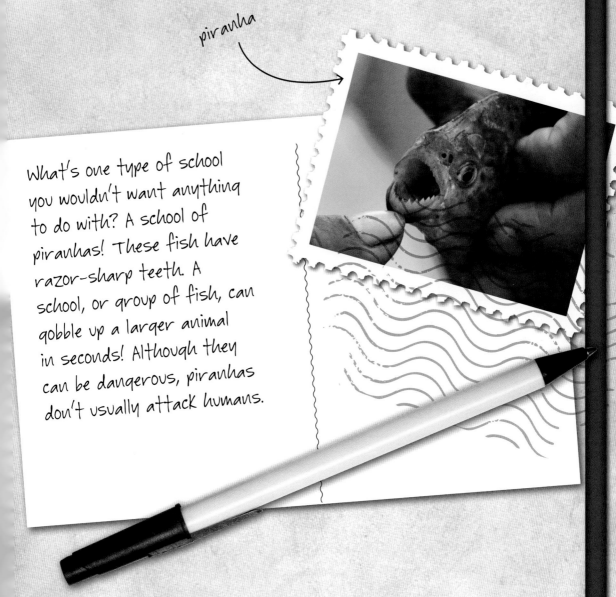

What's one type of school you wouldn't want anything to do with? A school of piranhas! These fish have razor-sharp teeth. A school, or group of fish, can gobble up a larger animal in seconds! Although they can be dangerous, piranhas don't usually attack humans.

➻ Large areas of rainforest have been destroyed to make room for cattle to graze.

Very few people live in the rainforest. There are not many roads. Unfortunately, that hasn't stopped people from destroying parts of it. **Deforestation** has become a problem as trees are cut down for lumber. They are also cleared for farming or to raise cattle.

Just south of the Amazon, you'll find the central western part of Brazil. The capital city, Brasília, is found here. It's also home to a large part of the Pantanal, the world's biggest wetland. It is approximately 10 times as large as the Florida Everglades.

The northeastern region of Brazil has a very beautiful coastal area that is lush and green. It is also the home of the *sertão*, a desert-like area. Very little can grow here. People who live in this area have to struggle to survive. They often move to bigger cities in order to find jobs.

Want to take a trip to Brazil during your summer vacation? You might want to bring a sweater. Why? Because it will be winter in Brazil! While most parts of Brazil don't ever get very cold, the coldest time of the year is between June and August. The warmest temperatures occur between December and February.

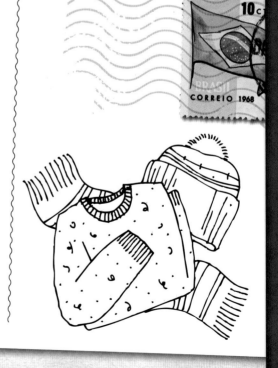

The southeastern part of the country is home to three of Brazil's biggest cities: São Paulo, Rio de Janeiro, and Belo Horizonte. São Paulo is the largest city in South America. This part of the country has a very mild climate. There is also enough rain to grow fruits, vegetables, and one of Brazil's most important crops: coffee.

The southern region is the only part of Brazil that has four seasons. You'll find huge flat plains called pampas. Here, Brazil's gauchos—or cowboys—herd cattle. One of the most amazing sights in southern Brazil is Iguaçu Falls. It is made up of more than 275 separate waterfalls!

↪ Iguaçu Falls' beautiful views make it a popular place for tourists to visit.

Brazil is made up of 26 states. There is also one federal district, which is where you'll find Brasília, the capital. Using a separate sheet of paper, trace the map. Use an atlas or find a map online and label each of the 26 states and Brasília. Do you notice that some states are small while others are large? Why do you think this might be?

BUSINESS AND GOVERNMENT IN BRAZIL

Sugarcane is one crop grown on plantations in Brazil.

How do people earn a living in Brazil? For many years, most people grew crops. When Brazil was a colony of Portugal (1500–1822), there were huge plantations. Most of the people who worked on them didn't choose their jobs. They were slaves brought from Africa. Even though Brazil became an independent country in 1822, slavery didn't end until 1888.

Throughout the 1900s, Brazil had both good and bad times. The economy was quite strong after World War I (1914–1918) and World War II (1939–1945). That's because Brazil had natural resources to make products and many other countries didn't. In the 1950s, Brazil worked hard to quickly become a more modern country.

Today, Brazilian farmers grow crops such as coffee, sugarcane, citrus, and soybeans. Workers also make clothing, shoes, and many different types of equipment. Some examples include cars and airplanes.

➻ Some Brazilians work in automobile factories.

•❖ Brazil's police officers provide many services to the country's citizens.

Although agriculture and **manufacturing** are important, most people do not earn their living in these areas. Approximately 20% of Brazilians grow or produce food. Roughly 14% make some kind of product. The other 66% of Brazilians are involved in service industries. This means they provide a service rather than make or grow something. Teachers and police officers are examples of people who work in service industries.

ACTIVITY

Bar graphs are a good way to compare different values. Make a bar graph to show how many people have jobs related to agriculture, making a product, or providing a service. Ask an adult for help if you need it. Use the percentages mentioned in this chapter. Which bars will be close in size? Which bar will be more than three times taller than the other two?

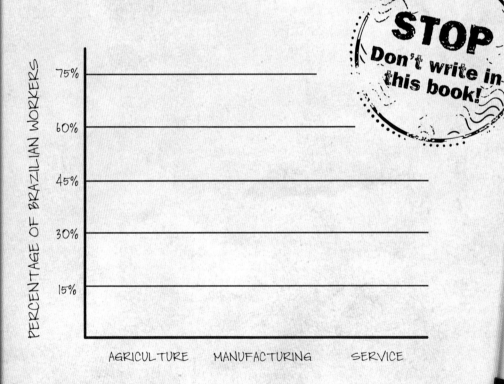

STOP
Don't write in this book!

PERCENTAGE OF BRAZILIAN WORKERS

75%

60%

45%

30%

15%

AGRICULTURE   MANUFACTURING   SERVICE

TYPE OF INDUSTRY

Jobs in Brazil have changed over time. So has the government. Brazil was once a colony ruled by the king of Portugal. When Brazil became independent, it had an emperor, which is a lot like a king. Brazil's first emperor was the king of Portugal's son.

The Brazilian unit of money is called the real (ray-AHL). The plural of real is reais. In 2010, one U.S. dollar was worth approximately 1.7 reais.

➜ Brazil's government is run from
the capital city of Brasilia.

When slavery ended in 1888, wealthy landowners
were upset. They worked with the army to force the
emperor out of power and created a new type of government called a republic. In a republic, the people are sup-
posed to choose their leaders. Unfortunately, this hasn't
always been true in Brazil. Many times, the government
of Brazil has been run by a **dictator**. The government
often took away people's freedoms and put them in jail.
In 1985, this type of government finally ended.

Today, the government of Brazil has three branches: executive, legislative, and judicial. The executive branch includes the president and vice president. They are elected by voters. The president serves a 4-year term and can be elected two times. He or she chooses a cabinet to help run the country.

Luiz Inácio Lula da Silva

In 2002, Brazilians elected their first **working-class** president: Luiz Inácio Lula da Silva. He is known as "Lula." Lula promised to try to make Brazil a better place for everyone, not just the rich. The Brazilian economy has improved since his election.

Officials in the legislative branch are also elected by the people. They help make the laws. The judicial branch helps interpret the laws.

Brazil's flag has a green background with a yellow diamond. There is a blue circle in the middle of the diamond. There are 27 stars in the circle, one for each state and one for the federal district. The grouping of the stars is special. They are arranged in the same way that they appeared in the sky on the night the republic of Brazil was created, November 15, 1889. There is a white band that stretches across the blue circle. It features Brazil's motto, Ordem e Progresso. or "Order and Progress."

MEET THE PEOPLE

Brazil's culture is a blend of many different ethnic backgrounds.

Many people describe Brazil as a melting pot. A melting pot is a place where the people come from different cultures and mix together to create something new. Many of Brazil's people are a mix of three ethnic groups: Amerindian, Portuguese, and African. Others have roots in Japan, Germany, Italy, Lebanon, and China.

Amerindian is the name for the millions of native people who first lived in Brazil. These native people came from many different tribes and spoke many different languages. They survived by fishing, hunting, and farming.

You might be surprised to know that Brazil has one of the world's largest Japanese populations outside of Japan!

❧ Amerindian culture is alive and well in some parts of Brazil.

Portuguese explorers came to Brazil in 1500. This meant big changes for the native people. The explorers brought new diseases that killed many of the Amerindians. They forced the Amerindians to work as slaves. They also forced them to learn the Portuguese language and way of dressing.

As the plantations grew, the Portuguese needed more people to work on them. They began to bring Africans to Brazil as slaves. The cultures of the Amerindians, Portuguese, and Africans mixed almost immediately.

Today, it is easy to see the many ways that these groups have influenced one another. One good example is the way Brazilians look. They have a wide variety of skin, hair, and eye colors.

Brazilian music reflects a mix of different cultures, too. The samba is the most popular dance in Brazil. It has its roots in Africa. Brazilian musical styles include *bossa nova*, *frevo*, *forró*, and *chorinho*.

The blend of different ethnic backgrounds means that Brazilians often look very different from one other.

☛ Many different kinds of churches can be seen throughout Brazil.

Religion is another example of how different cultures influence one another in Brazil. Approximately 75% of Brazilians are Catholic. The Portuguese introduced Catholicism to Brazil. But many Catholics in Brazil add elements from African and Amerindian religions.

Likewise, some Brazilians practice religions with African roots that have taken on aspects of Catholicism and other beliefs. There is also a growing number of Protestants in Brazil.

The Christ the Redeemer statue in Rio de Janeiro is one of the world's most famous religious symbols. It is 125 feet (38.1 m) tall, including the pedestal.

Portuguese is Brazil's official language. Brazil is one of the few countries in South America where Spanish isn't the main language.

PORTUGUESE

Can you match the Portuguese words to their English translations? Hint: if you know any Spanish, you might have an easier time! See below for the answers.

Portuguese	English
1. Um (OOM)	a. Four
2. Quatro (KWAH-troh)	b. One
3. Cinco (SINK-oh)	c. Five
4. Dois (DOYZ)	d. Three
5. Três (TRAYZ)	e. Two

STOP Don't write in this book!

Answers: 1-b; 2-a; 3-c; 4-e; 5-d

Approximately 80% of Brazilians live in cities. Many people live in crowded **slums** called *favelas*. Some of the most well-known slums are in São Paulo and Rio de Janeiro. In Rio the rich people have houses in the flat areas, especially near the beaches. The poor people live in the hills. The people in the hills live in shacks and don't have running water. Poverty is a challenge that the people of Brazil are trying to overcome.

In big cities, some children live on the streets in dangerous conditions. Different groups try to help these children, but it is difficult because there are so many of them.

CORREIO 1968

In Brazil, school is **mandatory** for children between the ages of 7 and 14. But not all children get to attend. Many poor families need their children to earn money or to help at home. In some places, children only go to school for half of the day. Approximately 89% of the people in Brazil know how to read. Some children continue to go to school after the age of 14, but many do not. Those who do go on to secondary school—known as high school in the United States—attend from the ages of 15 to 17. Some students attend a university after this, but they must first take a very difficult exam.

LET'S CELEBRATE!

→ People flood Brazil's streets during the celebration of Carnaval.

The people of Brazil love to have a good time. One of their most famous and popular celebrations is *Carnaval*. This is a giant outdoor party that occurs each year in the days before Lent begins. Lent is the period of time before Easter. This is when Christians get ready for the celebration of Easter by praying, giving to others, and making sacrifices such as giving up favorite foods.

During Carnaval, people dress up in costumes and masks. There is music and dancing. There are also huge parades with floats. One of the most famous parades is in Rio de Janeiro. It features samba performers. People from different neighborhoods compete to see who has the best dancers, music, and costumes. Each neighborhood group is called a "Samba School." The cities of Salvador and Olinda also have famous Carnaval celebrations. The music at these celebrations is different from the music played in Rio de Janeiro.

Some people wear elaborate masks and costumes during Carnaval.

How about celebrating Carnaval with a simple noisemaker?

Materials:
- 2 sturdy plastic or paper cups (both cups should be the same size)
- ¼ to ½ cup of any combination of the following: uncooked rice, uncooked beans or lentils, uncooked macaroni
- Masking tape

Instructions:
1. Take one of the cups and pour your mixture of uncooked rice, beans, lentils, or macaroni into it.

Continued
on the
following page

2. Set the cup on a flat work surface.

3. Set the rim of the second cup on top of the rim of the first cup.

4. Wrap tape completely around the edges to hold the cups together. Be sure to create a tight seal so your materials don't fall out.

Make a noisemaker for each of your friends so you can celebrate together. Then put on some lively music, shake your noisemakers, and create your own Carnaval!

→ Brazilians hold large parties along the beach to celebrate Iemanjá.

Christmas is an important holiday in Brazil. Christians celebrate the birth of Jesus Christ on Christmas Day, which is December 25. People of many beliefs enjoy a visit from Papai Noel, the Brazilian Santa Claus!

Iemanjá is a Brazilian celebration that honors the goddess of the sea. It is celebrated on December 31 in Rio de Janeiro and February 2 in Bahia. During this festival, people head to the beaches to offer gifts. Some put their offerings on small boats. They believe that if the boats sink, the goddess has accepted their gifts and will bring them good things in the coming year. If the boats return, it means the goddess has refused the gifts.

On July 2, people who live in the Northeast part of Brazil celebrate the Independence of Bahia.

On April 21, the people of Brazil celebrate Tiradentes Day. This holiday is in memory of Joaquim José da Silva Xavier, a dentist who went by the name Tiradentes. Tiradentes led an unsuccessful **rebellion** for Brazil's independence.

September 7 is Independence Day in Brazil. This date marks Brazil's independence from Portugal in 1822.

What do children in Brazil like to do for fun? Most of them play *futebol*. You might know this game as soccer. Brazil takes this sport very seriously. The national soccer team has won the World Cup many times. Pelé was a Brazilian soccer player in the 1960s. Many people believe that he was the best soccer player of all time. In 2016, Brazil will host the World Cup competition.

◆ Brazil's national soccer team has many fans.

Capoeira is also a popular activity. It combines martial arts and dance. Many people believe that Capoeira was originally a way for slaves to train to fight so they could escape. The training was disguised as a dance! It has since become popular around the world.

In 2009, Rio de Janeiro was chosen to be the host city for the 2016 Summer Olympics. This will be the first time a South American country hosts the Olympic Games.

These are some of Brazil's national holidays:

January 1	New Year's Day
February or March	Carnaval
April 21	Tiradentes Day
May 1	Labor Day
May or June	Corpus Christi
September 7	Independence Day
October 12	Nossa Senhora Aparecida (the patron saint of Brazil)
November 2	All Souls' Day
November 15	Proclamation of the Republic Day
December 25	Christmas

Brazil has more than 4,000 miles (6,437.4 km) of coastline and warm temperatures for much of the year. It's no surprise, then, that Brazilians who live in coastal areas spend a lot of time at the beach. They enjoy activities such as surfing, windsurfing, and swimming.

CHAPTER FIVE

TIME TO EAT!

➥ Shrimp is an ingredient in many Brazilian dishes.

What types of food do you think are popular in Brazil? Remember that the country is a melting pot. You shouldn't be surprised, then, to learn that foods from all over the world can be found in Brazil. Each region has it own specialties. People who live near the coast, for example, eat a lot of seafood.

Manioc is common in Brazil. Parts of this tropical plant can be cooked and eaten like a potato or turned into flour. People who make manioc flour must know what they're doing. Why? The plant's roots are poisonous! The flour has to be made in a special way to remove the poison.

manioc

Many Brazilian dishes come from Portuguese, African, and Amerindian cultures. The Portuguese brought coffee and a love of desserts to Brazil. African cooks contributed spicy dishes using coconut milk, peppers, and *dendê* oil. Dendê oil is a bitter oil that comes from an African palm tree. Amerindians used foods found in Brazil, including sweet potatoes, corn, and seafood.

Gauchos like to make *churrasco*, or barbeque. It is traditionally served on big skewers, which are metal sticks.

If you go to someone's house for dinner, you might be served a delicious stew called *feijoada*. This stew usually has black beans, rice, and meat. Every family has its own special version.

Many Brazilian families enjoy eating the stew known as feijoada.

→ Sodas made with guarana are popular in Brazil.

With a tropical climate in most places, fruit is available all year. Fruit juices are very popular. A soda made from *guaraná* fruit is a favorite drink. Be careful! This soda contains more caffeine than a cup of coffee.

If you travel to Brazil, you'll want to brush up on your table manners. Keep your elbows off the table. Be sure to eat most things with a knife and fork. Instead of switching your knife and fork from one hand to the other, keep the fork in your left hand and the knife in your right.

Lunch is the largest meal of the day for most Brazilians.

Breakfast is usually a small meal in Brazil. Lunch is the biggest meal of the day. At lunch, people relax and enjoy dining with family and friends. Sometimes people will take hours to eat lunch. Dinner may be served late in big cities. Don't be surprised if you get a dinner invitation for 9:00 at night!

Do you like French toast? If so, you'll love the Brazilian version. It is served at Christmas in certain regions. This recipe requires the use of a stove. Ask an adult for help when heating anything.

Holiday Rabanada

INGREDIENTS

1 tablespoon (12 gm) sugar

¾ cup (177 ml) milk

2 large eggs

8 slices of bread

½ stick butter

½ cup (65 gm) powdered sugar

1 teaspoon (2.5 gm) cinnamon

Instructions are on the following page →

Instructions:

1. Combine the sugar, milk, and eggs in a large bowl. Use a fork or a whisk to mix them together. Be careful whenever handling raw eggs. Be sure to wash your hands and clean your work surface when you are finished cooking.

2. Heat the pan over medium heat. Add the butter to the pan. When the butter is melted, you're ready to cook. Be sure the butter doesn't burn.

3. Place the pieces of bread in the bowl. Let them soak until the bread is coated with the egg mixture. Using a spatula, carefully turn over each piece of bread. Let the bread soak on the other side. You probably won't be able to soak every piece at once. Soak the bread in batches of a few pieces at a time.

4. Use the spatula to lift each piece of bread and place it carefully in the hot pan. Have an adult help you. Cook the number of pieces of bread that will comfortably fit into the pan at one time. Make sure you have space to flip them over!

5. After 1 to 2 minutes, use the spatula to check the color of the side of bread touching the pan. When it is golden brown, flip it over and cook the other side.

6. When the second side is golden, remove the rabanada from the pan. Cook any remaining bread slices in the same way.

7. Sprinkle the cooked slices with powdered sugar and cinnamon.

Call your family to breakfast and enjoy!

Brazil is big. Brazil is booming. Brazil is beautiful. You could spend a lifetime exploring all of the treasures this amazing country has to offer. Happy travels!

➥ What part of Brazil would you like to explore first?

GLOSSARY

deforestation (dee-for-uh-STAY-shuhn) the cutting down of forests

dictator (DIK-tay-tur) a person who has complete control of a government

federal (FED-ur-uhl) having to do with a system in which states have their own governments but are also united under one central power

mandatory (MAN-duh-tor-ee) required

manufacturing (man-yuh-FAK-chuh-ring) the making of products, often with the use of equipment

rebellion (rih-BEL-yuhn) a fight or struggle against someone who is in control

slums (SLUHMZ) very poor, crowded, and rundown housing areas in a city

working-class (WURK-ing-KLASS) having to do with workers who are paid by the hour, often for jobs requiring little training

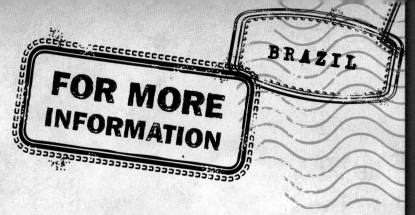

FOR MORE INFORMATION

Books

Heinrichs, Ann. *Brazil*. New York: Children's Press, 2008.

Koponen, Libby. *South America*. New York: Children's Press, 2009.

Walters, Tara. *Brazil*. New York: Children's Press, 2008.

Web Sites

Central Intelligence Agency—The World Factbook: Brazil
www.cia.gov/library/publications/the-world-factbook/geos/br.html
This is a great resource for information about Brazil's geography, economy, and more.

National Geographic Kids—Brazil
kids.nationalgeographic.com/Places/Find/Brazil
Here you'll find amazing facts and photos of Brazil.

TIME for Kids—Brazil
www.timeforkids.com/TFK/kids/hh/goplaces/main/0,28375,635502,00.html
Check out this site for Portuguese phrases, information about Brazil's different regions, and much more.

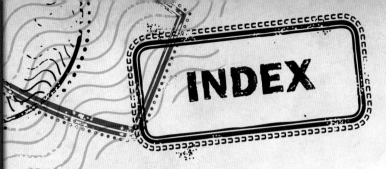

INDEX

activities, 12, 16, 27, 31–32, 43–44
African people, 13, 21, 24, 25, 39
agriculture, 8, 10, 14, 15
Amazon River, 6
Amerindian people, 21, 22, 23, 24, 25, 39
animals, 4, 7, 8, 11

Bahia, 33
Belo Horizonte, 10
borders, 5
Brasília, 9, 12

capital city, 9, 12
capoeira (martial art), 36
Carnaval celebration, 29–30, 31–32, 37
cattle, 8, 11
central western region, 5, 9
Christ the Redeemer statue, 26
cities, 9, 10, 12, 26, 27, 28, 30, 33, 36, 42
climate, 9, 10, 11, 41
coastline, 9, 37, 38
colonies, 13, 17

dancing, 26, 30, 36
deforestation, 8
dictators, 18

economy, 14, 19
education, 28
elections, 18, 19, 20
elevation, 6
emperors, 17, 18
ethnic groups, 21–24, 25, 39
executive branch of government, 19

favelas (slums), 27
federal district, 12, 20
flag, 20
foods, 15, 29, 38–42, 43–44
forests, 4, 7–8
futebol (soccer), 35

gauchos, 11, 40

holidays, 29–30, 33–34, 37

Iemanjá, 33
Iguaçu Falls, 11
independence, 13, 17, 34

Japanese people, 21, 22
jobs, 9, 13, 15, 16, 17
judicial branch of government, 19, 20

land area, 5
languages, 22, 23, 27
laws, 20
legislative branch of government, 19, 20
location, 5
Lula da Silva, Luiz Inácio, 19
lumber industry, 8

manufacturing, 14, 15
maps, 5, 12
marine life, 7, 22
money, 17, 28
motto, 20
music, 26, 30
natural resources, 14
northeastern region, 5, 9
northern region, 5, 6

pampas area, 11
Pantanal wetland, 9
Pelé, 35
Pico da Neblina, 6
plantations, 13, 24
plants, 4, 7, 39
Portugal, 13, 17, 34
Portuguese language, 27
Portuguese people, 21, 23–24, 25, 39
poverty, 27
presidents, 19

rainforests, 4, 7–8
religion, 25, 26, 29, 33
republics, 18
Rio de Janeiro, 10, 26, 27, 30, 33, 36

"Samba Schools," 30
São Paulo, 10, 27
sertão area, 9
service industries, 15
slavery, 13, 18, 23, 24, 36
southeastern region, 5, 10
southern region, 5, 11
sports, 35–36, 37
states, 12, 20

Tiradentes, 34

World War I, 14
World War II, 14

ABOUT THE AUTHOR
Vicky Franchino wanted to learn more about Brazil after it was chosen to host the 2016 Olympic Games. Now that she's learned more, she wants to visit Brazil—or at least eat Brazilian food! Vicky lives in Madison, Wisconsin, with her family and enjoys learning about and visiting new places.